If you wish to explore Norfolk, look out for these tit

Available at the time of printing.

The 'Albums' series

A Mundesley Album
A Cromer Album
A Sheringham Album
Sheringham — a Century of Change

The 'Norfolk Origins' series

Hunters to First Farmers
Roads and Tracks
Celtic Fire and Roman Rule

The 'East Anglian Memories' series

Those Seaside Days

Local history booklets

Great Yarmouth — History, Herrings and Holidays
Fakenham — Town on the Wensum
Holt — Historical Market Town
Coltishall — Heyday of a Broadland Village
Caister — 2000 Years a Village
The Cromer Lifeboats
Weybourne — Peaceful Mirror of a Turbulent Past
Have You Heard about Blakeney?
Salthouse — Village of Character and History
Cley — Living with Memories of Greatness
Poppyland — Strands of Norfolk History
The Hunstanton Lifeboats
Palling — A History Shaped by the Sea
Caister — Beach Boats and Beachmen

General Titles

His Majesty's Late Ship the Invincible
The Birds of Sheringham
East Anglia on Film

Many more titles are in preparation.
For a current list, ask at your bookshop or send an S.A.E. to
Poppyland Publishing, 13, Kings Arms Street, North Walsham, Norfolk NR28 9JX

Cover photo: The 'Poppy Line' gives the opportunity to travel by steam train between Sheringham and Weybourne. Work has now commenced on extending the line to the boundaries of Holt. (Photo: North Norfolk Railway)

© Carol Spero and Poppyland Publishing
Printed and bound by Speedprint Design, Spalding, Lincolnshire
Cover design and illustrations by Deeprose Design, Spalding, Lincolnshire
Typesetting by PTPS, Norwich
First Published 1987
ISBN: 0 946148 25 2

"" TAKING THE CHILDREN TOO...""

A book for the family
exploring Norwich & Norfolk

Poppyland Publishing

Carol Spero

Contents

The author offers grateful acknowledgements to the East Anglian Tourist Board and to British Rail for their co-operation in preparing this book, and also to Mr.and Mrs.Julian Spence for their kindness and assistance in the research.

Occasional reference has been made to such features as 'safe for bathing'. This is intended to be helpful, but you are strongly advised always to take local advice on such matters. Some bathing places are safe at one state of the tide and not at others. Many Norfolk beaches are covered by lifeguards during the summer, and they can always supply helpful advice. Likewise, the coastguards are able to assist. A number of beaches also have a flag system to indicate whether or not bathing is 'safe' and there will be posters explaining the meanings of the flags.

Photographic Acknowledgements: Poppyland Photos 6,12,17,21,36,46; Reckitt and Coleman Ltd. 9; Great Yarmouth Publicity Department 13; Peter Bower 25; Shire Horse Centre 28; Norfolk Wildlife Park 29; Peter Bird, Geggie Partners 33; Langham Glass House 34

INTRODUCTION

If you're a loving parent you already know that your own long-awaited visit to some beautiful or by-gone place may not be your six-year-old's idea of a great day out. Similarly there's a limit to the time any grown-up will smilingly endure hanging around playgrounds, sandpits, toy castles and toy trains, even in the most idyllic setting.

But if you can gaze out to sea, high from some ivy-hung battlement, awaiting ghostly hordes to come sailing over the horizon, or imagine a knight in armour shadowed at every bend of the stairs as you climb some deserted tower, or if you can chuff all together through charming countryside in a shining wagon pulled by a real, though miniature steam engine, it's a different matter. And a visit to a historic house stacked with the toys and games that children actually played with hundreds of years ago can be an unforgettable experience, both for a small child - and you.

Sightseeing for children which will also give the grown-ups a good time needs a little organisation, that's all -perhaps with a book like this in your hand. It's not exactly a guide-book, however, more a tribute to one person's love for a part of East Anglia. So you may find some unusual lingerings, omissions, discoveries because East Anglia has a magic which is very personal, and it casts its spell quite differently on every individual.

Children are explorers by nature. They also love mysteries, and some of the subjects and places mentioned here need a sense of adventure and imagination to make them come to life. Commercially-made amusements have not, on the whole, been included although there are some important exceptions.

Norwich has been picked as the main centre because it's a good idea to have somewhere richly endowed from where to make your sorties, especially if you are using local buses and trains. It's a nice safe feeling to have somewhere solid to come back to at night, and Norwich is a treasure-house itself, with myriad things that children will love doing, seeing and experiencing. So even if it rains you will always find plenty of diversion and enjoyment there.

The book radiates from that city in most directions, the longest distance being about thirty miles, so that anywhere can be comfortably visited in a day or even a half-day. However, there are some delectable locations, such as the area around Wells-next-the-Sea, where it would be well worth spending a night or so.

Nor do you necessarily need a car, for many places mentioned here can be reached easily from the city centre by using local transport, especially the little pay-trains. However, there are some trips which can only be done it you have your own four wheels.

Londoners can whizz up to Norwich in two hours on British Rail, and the pay-trains that cover the seaside and country from there are quick and fun to travel on. You can discover things this way that you might very well miss if you went by car. Journeying to Great Yarmouth on the Wherry Line, for instance, is the only way I know where you can observe small boats sailing along what appear to be the the the middle of fields, their masts sticking up out of the reeds like lollipop sticks.

A couple of Ordnance Survey maps will cover most of the places mentioned in the text. The book is arranged in chapters by topic, so that you can plan your day according to your mood. In fact the book has been envisaged to include things that most children between the ages of, say, five and fifteen will delight in without boring their parents because each subject covered has something that should appeal to every member of the family from granny down.

Enjoy yourselves!

Norwich Castle looks down on the city on all sides. You can visit it as a castle or a museum – see page 15. Look out for special children's events in the schools holidays.

NORWICH

Gracious Norwich is a city which contains as much delight for children as it does for grown-ups. It's invigorating, varied and beautiful. If you want to spend all morning in W.H.Smith's or Woolworths, consuming sticky buns or poking around the kalaiedoscopic market-stalls you can. You can also explore cobbled streets and alleys on foot, or sail past them as far as tranquil and green Broadland. You can amuse yourself with the same pastimes that Victorian children did, observe at close range the animals and birds of East Anglia in replicas of their natural habitat. You can see how textiles were produced and printed, or follow the shoemaker's craft from early times. and practically every museum and place of interest now has its own gift shop where pocket money, even the most modest, can be interestingly spent. Let's start with some of these.

The **CASTLE MUSEUM GIFTSHOP** which you pass through anyway on your visit to the enchantments of Norwich Castle (fully described on page 15), sells all sorts of hard and paperback publications on local wild life. Also Nature Trail books, tracing sheets, cut-out castles and prints of birds and animals to colour. There are brightly painted animal jigsaws, rubbers, pencils, replicas of Roman coins and attractive and funny postcards for the frugal and there's also a cafeteria which offers individual sweets for mere pennies, as well as the more usual fizzy drinks and so on.

The large **CATHEDRAL SHOP** has plenty of good quality souvenirs for children - as well as pricier things for grown-ups - like lavender sachets and mini-soaps, Cathedral badges and pencils and other small items carrying the Cathedral's picture. The handsome **MUSTARD SHOP** in Bridewell Alley, which is also a tiny Mustard Museum, sells every blend of Colman's Mustard you've ever heard of, and some you haven't, but it also includes attractive souvenirs to suit small pockets like bookmarks and pencils and more mustardy things like mustard-spoons, pots and old-fashioned Colman's picture-postcards.

Local shops come and go, but here are a few especially unusual ones, open at the time of writing.

ELM HILL CRAFTS SHOP on a cobbled corner of that lovingly preserved area has a headspinning array of little objects on which to lavish even a few pennies, like tiny bead-boxes and note-books, purses, matchbox toys, as well as other more expensive gifts. Also on Elm Hill is **THE GAMES ROOM**. Entirely devoted to that absorbing subject, there are new games, ancient games, war games and books about games, while battalions of lead soldiers in authentic uniform await the call to some far-gone battle.

HOVELLS on the corner of Bedford Street and Bridewell Alley, near the Mustard Shop, established since 1860, is unlikely to have moved by the time you read this. Rapidly expanding, it sells - mainly - attractive caneware of every kind from tiny inexpensive posy-baskets, straw dolls and animals to full-scale furniture. And in the narrow streets around the ancient Maddermarket, like Pottergate and Bedford Street, you will find lots of eye-catching small shops bursting with unusual things for youngsters to give, wear, use, eat and play with. In this part of the city there are also bright little eateries very often run by young people, who know how to provide nourishing and imaginative food at sensible prices.

At the **SATURDAY CRAFT MARKET** in St. Andrew's and Blackfriars Halls at the top of Elm Hill, there are always original hand-crafted toys, dolls, boxes, fun-brooches and handmade children's clothes, all of a high standard. If you're looking for something you are unlikely to see anywhere else, this is the place to go. It's also where to stop for home-baked cakes with coffee, or a light lunch in the spacious **CRYPT COFFEE BAR**.

Now for Museums. **STRANGER'S HALL**, Charing Cross, one of the most lovely and historic buildings in Norwich is as much a charmer for children as for grown-ups. It's a veritable time-warp for here you can see, and very often walk right into, rooms furnished in every period from the sixteenth century on. There's a Victorian sitting-room with all its cluttery furniture - foot warmers and all - and a Victorian papa's dressing room, where the new baby slept, together with tin bath, brass hot-water jug and a handsome wooden seat commode decorated in blue and white porcelain.

But best of all is the Toy Room, dominated by a real Punch and Judy booth crowded with authentic characters. There are china and wax dolls of every kind, both splendidly attired and humbly wooden and naked. There are dolls' houses furnished in fascinating detail, magic lanterns, stereoscopes and pretty little peep shows through which you may look at the same scenes as their Victorian owners once viewed. And there are spelling books, ABCs and games of the seventeen hundreds.

The **BRIDEWELL MUSEUM** in Bridewell Alley, near the Mustard Shop again, is as much a journey into nostalgia as of consuming interest to anyone who loves finding out how things work. You will find some absorbing examples of Norfolk crafts and industries at every stage of production: dyeing, textile printing, shoe-making. Also a wonderful jumble of objects in common use in the 1930s and 1940s, such as a vicious looking permanent waving machine dangling with electric heaters, cheek by jowl with an old wooden aeroplane screw and an early fridge. There are builder's carts, grocery bikes with huge baskets, milk dreys , some magnificent Golden Grasshopper, Anchor and Swan shop and pub signs, and several examples of the materials used to build houses in North Norfolk: pebble, flint, and the thatch from reedy river banks. A splendid collection.

The Mustard Shop is tucked away in Bridewell Alley, and is a place for you and the family to call – even if you don't like mustard!

We have already mentioned the Cathedral shop; perhaps we should have mentioned the **CATHEDRAL** first! What will surely fascinate the young and sharp-eyed are the various goings-on among the four hundred mediaeval 'bosses' way up in the vaulted roof and in the cloisters, where you get a better view. The bosses are tiny figures and scenes, mainly religious but also of local people, animals and birds. Some depict in great detail various weird and even nightmarish happenings, such as the wicked being cast into Hell - very frightening! Others are simply delightful and amusing representations of trades and callings, such as a stonemason at work, a windmill with the miller, Noah's Ark with all the animals, birds and people peeping out, and an engaging owl in a pear tree. Colour postcards of some of the bosses are on sale in the Cathedral shop (not open on Sundays) so you can examine these intriguing examples of church decoration at your leisure.

The **CATHEDRAL CLOSE** is probably the most charming and the broadest in England. Flanked by some handsome old houses with long flowery gardens and little enclaves where others, more ancient, huddle like gossiping old women, it's a pleasure to stroll by wide lawns dancing with early summer blossom. Follow the pathway past Norwich School playing field as far as Pull's Ferry - the ancient watergate to the Cathedral Close - and when you get there, look back at the Cathedral spire, its tip so fine it almost disappears into Heaven. If you turn right at Pull's Ferry, within a minute or so you'll be on the banks of the River Wensum and on your way along the towpath to the main road and then the station where you can take a boat through old Norwich back to cobbled Elm Hill. Or you can turn left instead at the Ferry and follow the river bank on foot all the way round round to the medieval heart of the city. It's a walk full of colour and interest and it takes about half an hour.

Boat trips along the Wensum are a pleasant thing to do for the whole family on a sunny Sunday. There are light snacks and a loo on board these **SOUTHERN RIVER STEAMERS** and the trip, of which there is more than one on Sundays, only takes an hour. You start by the palatial dome of Thorpe Railway Station, and as you progress you observe the city, warts and all. Gliding past the Colman's Mustard Factory, with the Canaries' football stadium opposite, you eventually emerge from beneath bridges old and new to placid reed-fringed water where you might spot a nesting bird, and where the woodland spreads her skirts down to green banks peppered with the homes of wild creatures like a scene from "The Wind in the Willows". Then you are at the beginning of Broadland itself where everyone, including the dog, seem out for a day on the river. On your return you will perceive once more the industrial face of Norwich, the ravishing Cathedral spire, through the long watery tresses of willows, until passing pretty Pull's Ferry again you reach Elm Hill where you find the city at its most ancient and charming - and disembark.

PIZZA ONE AND PANCAKES TWO in Tombland, a step or so away and right outside the Cathedral Walls, is run by a group of energetic young people and is open all day on a Sunday. A paradise for greedies of all ages, including vegetarians, they offer huge ices and the most exotic — or the most simple - crepes, and help you put together your own pizza creations. But they'll cheerfully serve a single apple-juice if that's all you or your loved ones want. Prices are moderate for such luscious food. A short step away and round the corner into London Street, you will find **LLOYD'S RESTAURANT**, where you can enjoy top quality full meals at very reasonable prices, or something lighter but equally delicious. The special pleasure is that as soon as the weather permits, tables and chairs are moved out into the central area of London Street - don't worry, it is pedestrianised! - and your coffee or meal will be served to you there.

Many redundant churches in East Anglia are now put to other good use and continue to nourish the creative spirit. Norwich has more than one such, and the little medieval church of St. James, Whitefriars (about four hundred yards from the Cathedral over Whitefriars Bridge) has been converted to house the **NORWICH PUPPET THEATRE**. For many years it was the home of the internationally famous Da Silva Puppet Company, and the present performers put on a constant programme of delight to children of all ages: shows, plays, demonstrations of puppetry. Programmes are available from the Norwich Tourist Office. And in **CINEMA CITY** in St.Andrew's Street, regular children's matinees are held at 2.30 on Saturdays during term-time, while throughout the summer holidays there are special children's programmes to please all tastes.

CASTLE MUSEUM Open Monday-Saturday 10a.m.-5p.m., Sunday 2-5p.m. Closed Good Friday, 23-26 December, New Year's Day.

STRANGERS' HALL MUSEUM Open Monday-Saturday 10a.m.-5p.m. Closed Sunday, Good Friday, 23-26 December, New Year.

BRIDEWELL MUSEUM Open Monday-Saturday 10a.m.-5p.m. Closed Sunday, Good Friday, 23-26 December, New Year.

SOUTHERN RIVER STEAMERS 1 to 2 hour river trips daily, May-September, from Elm Hill.

TO GREAT YARMOUTH THROUGH A LAND OF WINDMILLS

By far the nicest way to visit Great Yarmouth from Norwich is by the little pay-train, for by this route you enter a different world; a journey, though short, that first wanders prettily along the river, then leads you through marshlands to a Dutch landscape of windmills which stand like ghosts among the shadowy water meadows, themselves etched with inlets so well-concealed that here and there the masts of small craft seem to be sailing through the flat fields.

Many of the mills - the general opinion is that they are all called mills, even though many pumped water rather than milled corn - are now sail-less, like huge pepper-pots. One which has been thoroughly restored is **BERNEY ARMS MILL**, the tallest marsh mill on the Norfolk Broads, and this you pass on the way. The mill can be seen to great advantage from the New Cut at Reedham, but if you like you can alight from the train at Berney Arms Halt, perhaps on your return from Great Yarmouth, and approaching across fields, take a closer look at it and at the exhibition of windmills inside.

But back to Great Yarmouth where you are bound. The town can be all you expect: a fun place pure and simple, with candy-floss and caravans, big dippers and blowy walks along the prom, fish and chips, waxworks, winter gardens and two hundred glorious acres of sand. However if you've a mind you can discover a completely other Yarmouth, just as exciting in its way but full of unexpected delights.

In that case, when you get off the train cross the old iron bridge and, ignoring the signs to the left which say "Town Centre," continue straight ahead along the North Quay until you come to the blue bridge which crossed the South Quay. Stop and look to the left towards the nineteenth century Town Hall fronted by a busy tree-lined space framed with buildings of all periods. Cross to the far side of the quay and view the building of the old town over the water through a delicate tracery of masts and sails. So strong is the Dutch, or perhaps the Flemish, influence that you may wonder if you are in England at all, or have been transported by magic to the heart of some lively foreign port!

On the quayside itself, heavy with craft of every kind, it's a thoroughly salty scene. Here you will find continental vessels and others from the north of

England, at rest before steaming up to Norwich, small boats journeying busily along the inland waterways, and bobbing pleasure craft and yachtsmen en route to holidays on the Broads. You can stand and watch for hours, absorbing the romance of distant lands, and now and again catching the echoes of foreign tongues.

It is in this section of the old town that you will find remains of the "Rows," narrow passageways , running at right angles to the quay. Here sailors and fishermen, as well as rich merchants lived in medieval times. Many of the houses were destroyed by war-time bombs, but one that has been restored is the **OLD MERCHANT'S HOUSE**, reached along South Quay. It's a time-warp of twisting stairways and enchainements of low-ceilinged rooms, some of which have been restored to their original condition. A great opportunity to recapture the atmosphere in which both social groups lived in that part of the town.

By looking back across the river you can see the Ice House, just south of the bridge. Thankfully it has been carefully restored in recent years; its thick walls and thatch once preserved ice brought during the winter months from Scandinavia or the Broads until it was required by the fishing vessels. It is just one of the reminders of the many aspects of Great Yarmouth's past.

We don't promise you'll find the brig 'Royalist' moored in Yarmouth harbour, but you'll always find a selection of interesting vessels.

The traditional beach entertainments are available at Great Yarmouth, as well as the kind of alternatives suggested on these pages.

The **ELIZABETHAN HOUSE MUSEUM** nearby - let by the National Trust to Norfolk Museum Service - is another, with its richly-panelled rooms, imposing furniture and carved fireplaces, together with simple domestic objects of the period. There's a Victorian kitchen too, for this is a museum of local life from varying times, and children will love the collection of flat-irons and the mangles whose handles they can turn in the scullery. Best of all - the toy room with its collection of Victorian toys and games. Here you'll find an enormous dolls' house, regiments of lead soldiers, more than one Noah's Ark with animals, a magic lantern and a rather nasty squirrels' tea party in a glass case, all the squirrels being fine examples of the taxidermist's art.

Nearby there's an alcove which reveals a turn-of-the-century schoolmaster's desk complete with old fashioned nib pens and salt glaze inkpots, while among the writing and spelling books you will find a shaming Punishment Book, open for all to see. In the passage leading off this are some beautiful wood-carvings on the walls which depict scenes and characters from Dickens' books, done not so long ago by a local woodcarver, Henry Smith, who died in 1962.

13

The mediaeval **TOLHOUSE MUSEUM** is only a short step behind the South Quay in Tolhouse Street. Once the town's courthouse and gaol, the bloodthirsty will much enjoy a visit to the original dungeon with its four cells. Here can be found the books listing both the crimes and punishments meted out: "on suspicion of stealing 1 piece of rope value 6 pence" (remand) ..." a seaman engaged to serve on board the smack Regalia did unlawfully refuse to proceed to sea" (six weeks hard labour) and there are more crimes and punishments on show under glass for visitors to ponder over at their leisure. The Tolhouse has many other local history exhibits, and brass rubbings especially will find a visit worthwhile because this is also a centre for that most absorbing activity.

Anyone who has ever shed tears over the book "Black Beauty" will want to visit **ANNA SEWELL HOUSE** on Church Plain, just off the Market Place. In this attractive beamed and panelled little house, which has been restored to its seventeenth century condition, the authoress was born in 1820. Though it does not contain any of the authoresses's personal items any more, you can still see inside as it is now a pleasant tea-room where you can spend a restful hour enjoying home-made cakes in the shadow of her presence.

Incidentally, Anna Sewell died within six months of writing "Black Beauty" and only made £20 out of sales of a book which today is still bought in its millions all over the world!

After tea it won't take you long to retrace your steps to the present day by way of jazzy Marine Parade and all the fun of the fair, but even here you can enter another era if you wish by exploring the **MARITIME MUSEUM**, halfway along. Originally built in 1860 as a home for shipwrecked sailors the Museum provides a happy opportunity for anyone, young or old, to trace the seafaring heritage of the area. You will find the story of Great Yarmouth's herring industry with models from the fisheries, the history and development of ships and ship-building from the dug-out canoe to the hovercraft, and from Nelson to the Norfolk Broads today. There are ships in bottles, carved whale-tusks, objects brought back from famous polar expeditions and the story of wherries, windpumps and waterways.

BERNEY ARMS MILL Open 1 April-30 September daily 9.30am-6.30p.m.
OLD MERCHANT'S HOUSE Open April-Sept, Mon-Fri 9.30a.m.-6p.m.
ELIZABETHAN HOUSE MUSEUM, South Quay Open June-September daily (except Saturday). 10a.m.-1p.m., 2p.m.-5.30p.m. October-May, Monday-Friday only 10a.m.-1p.m., 2-5.30p.m.

TOLHOUSE MUSEUM, Tolhouse Street. Open October-May, Monday-Friday only, June-September daily (except Saturday) 10a.m.-1p.m., 2-5.30p.m.

MARITIME MUSEUM FOR EAST ANGLIA Open October-May, Monday-Friday 10a.m.-1p.m., 2-5.30p.m. June-September daily except Saturday, 10a.m.-5.30p.m.

CASTLES — AND THAT SORT OF THING

Castles and ruins that children will get the most out of are the ones that haven't been too perfectly restored. Perfection implies artifice - very nice and easy to enjoy but leaving little to the imagination.

Ruined places contain memories, shadows, secrets. They incorporate space and time imprinted with dramatic, splendid and often violent happenings. They are often isolated so that you can stand on some quiet mound and hear the sounds of long-gone battles on the air. Or from the remains of ramparts rooted in ivy, look down and imagine the feasting and revelry, the golden princesses, in a baronial hall below, while the wind blows around you.

So with the exception of Norwich Castle, (something unique) the places mentioned here are remains of castles and other ruins: walls, keeps, hillocks, tunnels and underground chambers that can be explored, run around and fantasised upon to the heart's content.

A visit to **NORWICH CASTLE** is perhaps the thing children will love best in this city of delights.

The Castle itself, poised austerely on its green mound, has the appearance of one you might see in a toyshop. This may be because it has been restored more than once and some bits look as though they could have been done yesterday, (actually part of the Castle was refaced in Bath stone in 1834).

The keep is vast enough for even the liveliest to feel free to wander around and examine the constantly changing exhibitions of Norfolk life and times beneath the blazing eyes of Snap the Dragon, a huge, bizarre head-dress used in mayoral processions since mediaeval times which hangs suspended in the air.

A visit to the dungeons, with a talk by a dungeon expert, is not to be missed and these are conveniently timed for the school holidays. Anyone can join in without booking, for a modest fee, and as well as the dungeons themselves you can see such gory exhibits as thumb-screws, irons, stocks and of course ducking-stools for garrulous wives.

Apart from the keep there is not much left inside the Castle, so the Rotunda which was built into the centre of it in recent times - all light wood and dove-grey galleries and stairways, containing myriad pleasures - was a happy thought. It provides hours of fascination for children as young as six years old, and also for grown-ups who will go mainly to see the eighteenth and nineteenth century Lowestoft porcelain and the paintings.

In fact the whole family could spend an entire morning or afternoon there (especially a rainy one) without getting bored, interspersed with inexpensive snacks in the ground floor cafeteria where there is plenty of leg-room. You could easily park the younger ones there enjoying fizzy drinks and biscuits while you go off to see the Cotmans and other products of the Norwich Painters' School, whose galleries lead directly off.

Small children will love the dioramas of Norfolk wild-life and habitat, marsh and coastline, in the ecology section - especially a brambly Norfolk loke where thay can spot rabbits, hedgehogs and a thrush enjoying a snail lunch.

There are collections of butterflies that look like fairies, others grand as princes from a Dulac picture-book; there are flower-sprays of sea-coral and exquisitely patterned shells and fossils. They will enjoy the stuffed tigers, polar-bears, giant turtles, the generous variety of British birds and their nests and eggs, as well as some dramatically depicted dioramas of Bronze and Iron Age domestic and working life.

And in a glass case upstairs labelled 'Horrid Murders' you can follow the true tale of Victorian murderer James Rush. There's his home at Potash Farm, the scene of the crime at Stanfield Hall, James Rush himself, and Norwich Castle where he was hanged - all commemorated in mantlepiece ornaments made of Staffordshire pottery. A creepy example of the Victorians' entrancement with the macabre.

The Museum Giftshop is an Aladdin's Cave of picture books to colour, nature trail books, jigsaw puzzles, realistic stones and fossils, brooches and badges - all at sensible prices. The nice thing about this shop (described further on page 7) is that a lot of the objects offered are unlikely to be found elsewhere in the country, so they make specially cherished gifts and souvenirs.

Both **BURGH CASTLE** and **CAISTER CASTLE** are not far from Great Yarmouth - only a short distance from Norwich, so they could make a pleasant day or half-day's holiday outing.

Remains of a Roman fort dating from about A.D.300 make up the massive ruins of Burgh Castle, an area of six acres enclosed by remains of walls nine feet thick and about fifteen feet high. It is situated on a wide arm of the sea overlooking the River Waveney and guarding Breydon. This once vast Roman fortress, dominating miles of shallow water framed by the woods of Norfolk, defended Britain against Saxon invaders. One can imagine fleets of war-galleys anchored there, and trading ships from Gaul and further afield sailing between here and Norwich. You stand in a quadrangle - haunted by such scenes -surrounded by three flint and brick walls, bits and pieces of which rise up in odd monster groups, looking across Breydon Water and the Halvergate marshes.

CAISTER CASTLE, about one mile inland from Caister-on-Sea, and mirrored in a moat, was built in the 1440's by Sir John Fastolf (or Falstaff) after he returned from fighting the French wars with a fortune of gold. With this booty he constructed the Castle, with its romantic curtain walls and tall tower,

Caister Castle and Motor Museum is a mile or so inland from the main village of Caister. The moat is more than just an attraction for visitors – it's home for some!

and there he spent the rest of his life. It is here that, after his death, many of the famous Paston letters were written, for the Castle then fell into the hand of that family.

From the ruins there is a magnificent view over the surrounding countryside, and in the grounds is a large motor museum, where you can see vehicles from as far back as 1893, right to the present time - including the first real motor-car in the world - the 1893 Panhard Levassor.

BUNGAY - just inside Suffolk - is a must, both for its castle, and for the fact that the town is one of the most beautiful and interesting within a bus-ride of Norwich.

There was a castle here before the Normans came and strengthened it, making the place even more defensible, for at one time it would have been at the head of a navigable river. Twin towers and enormous flint walls are all that now remain - but it's fun to explore because the best way of reaching some parts is by crawling through a mine gallery under the south-west corner of the ruins of the keep, crossing which are two small cuts. It is said that this was an unfinished sapper's tunnel excavated during Henry II's time in order to set fire to the timber shoring up the whole thing and thus causing the castle to collapse. The owner, turbulent baron Bigod, had rebelled against the King in 1174 and had refused to pay his dues, so the King ordered Bungay to be dismantled. However, the baron eventually paid up, the tunnelling ceased, and the castle was spared destruction.

GRIMES GRAVES, near **WEETING CASTLE**, need to be visited wearing old clothes and carrying a torch. They are situated a few miles from Thetford, which is a straightforward run from Norwich on the A11, and reveal one of the most fascinating aspects of East Anglia's past. Not only that - you can actually get inside!

Craters are believed to have existed here for four thousand years, and one was excavated during the last century, revealing the shaft and tunnels of a neolithic flint mine. More have been excavated since then, and at least one is open to the public so you can explore the tunnels and see some of the antler picks, which were lying there when the mines were first uncovered.

For Stone Age man, flint was the most useful tool, and the flints found here were of the finest quality. There were probably over seven hundred shafts to similar pits, and it's exciting to scramble down a ladder and see the marks of the very antler picks made by men working there four thousand years ago, fresh as though they had been made yesterday. You can crouch in these galleries like the miners did as they cut away patiently at the flint by the glow of tiny chalk carved lamps.

Why are Grimes Graves so called? Nobody knows.

The mines are situated in the parish of Weeting, whose castle ruins are moat-encircled and set in beautiful parkland. Call there on your way. It's free.

Very few people have heard about **THURSFORD CASTLE** - a mysterious place indeed, for it virtually does not exist, though it's marked on the Ordnance Survey map. You'll find it a few miles from Thursford Steam Museum (see page 24) but all there is to be seen is a rectangular, weed-grown space, bounded by a red brick wall in a small spinney. From time to time you will encounter an abandoned fireplace set in a wall, its mantle drooping sadly above...a trace of wallpaper...here and there a handsome arched window hidden among brambles. Opposite, across a path, stands a deserted chapel half-swathed in ivy, through which the empty eyes of windows, glass long gone, peer over the Castle site. There's a stone plaque: "Castle Paddock" inscribed in the chapel wall. Was Thursford Castle the name of some grandiose Victorian or Edwardian pile? Why - and when - was it abandoned? What went on behind the arched windows through which now only fingers of nettle and loose-strife beckon in the wind? It's stimulating to explore and conjecture, if only for half-an-hour or so. You are unlikely to come across another living soul, but this strange little place may well call you back and back.

NORWICH CASTLE MUSEUM Monday-Saturday 10a.m.-5p.m., Sunday 2p.m.-5p.m. Closed Good Friday, 23-26 December, New Year's Day.

CAISTER CASTLE Open daily during season (ex. Saturday) 10.30a.m.-5p.m.

BURGH CASTLE Open daily throughout the year, dawn to dusk.

BUNGAY CASTLE Open daily all year. Keyholders listed.

WEETING CASTLE GRIMES GRAVES Check opening times locally.

ALL SORTS OF MILLS

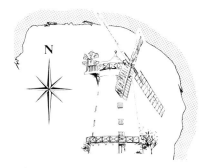

Mills, both wind and water, are signposts and symbols upon the flat landscape of rivery, marshy, north and north-east Norfolk. Watermills are thought to have been introduced into Britain by the innovative Romans, some being sited on tidal rivers so that they could be turned by the ebb and flow of the tide. But since the 12th century, where water power could not be used for grinding corn or for pumping water from marshy fens and broads, the wind was harnessed instead and put to work. When you explore a mill it's fascinating and romantic to realise that man has been using wind and water power in this way constantly since those times. It's fun spotting the various types, many of which are still in working order or have recently been restored.

There are three main sorts of windmill: the post mill, the tower mill and the smock mill. In Norfolk the word windmill is generally used even when it is actually a wind pump, this last term being applied to the modern form which has a small wheel like a fantail on a metal pylon, of which many are found in the marshy parts of Norfolk.

The post mill was built on four brick piers and a large central oak post. Sometimes this post consisted of a whole tree-trunk which was supported by an enormous cross of oak beams. The rest of the building could be rotated around the post so that the miller could turn his sails to catch the direction of the prevailing wind.

The tower mill - rather like a lighthouse - was developed during the 18th century and consisted of a brick or stone tower, usually round or octagonal. The sails were attached to the domed top of the tower and the movement from the sails was transmitted to the millstones through gear wheels.

Smock mills are perhaps the most charming, being either eight or twelve sided and built of wooden frames covered with clapboard. Only the top portion of the mill revolved like post mills. Smock mills were so-called because their sloping sides looked like the 19th century countryman's smock.

When you watch the huge sails and wheels and grinders at work, employing a rhythm and order which is so simple and yet so logical, you are experiencing something that has been part of man's creative instinct since earliest times - a sight both beautiful and comforting.

Working mills, where it's possible to go inside and see all the machinery operating, have a special allure for youngsters. Whether you are hooked on machinery or not, mills - both watery and windy - are unique, and exploring them, especially ones which are less frequented, has a sense of adventure and mystery unmatched by a visit to any other traditional building. Mills are wonderfully refreshing places from which to view the wide embrace of the Norfolk landscape - but they are fast disappearing, except as museum pieces - so make the most of them!

Very often mills incorporate small exhibitions of the miller's life and times. Some even sell the flour they grind, others have tea shops and souvenir shops attached; some stand stark and lonely, with no up-to-date trimmings in remote stretches of country near which wild birds and animals reside.

Starting nearest to Norwich **BERNEY ARMS MILL** is the tallest marsh mill on the Norfolk Broads. It's seen to great advantage from the New Cut at pretty little Reedham but you can also alight from the Norwich-Yarmouth pay-train at Berney Arms Halt itself, and walk over the flat fields to where the mill stands, black and aloof. It now belongs to English Heritage and is open to the public, so you can explore the inside and its interesting exhibition on windmills.

On the A47 from Norwich to Great Yarmouth you will find busy Acle and nearby the **STRACEY ARMS WINDPUMP**. Energetic windmill-lovers can climb ladders to the cap and inspect the brake wheels and gears, and there is also a fully-restored drainage pump. Exhibitions of photographs and history of Broadland windpumps are also on show at Stracey Arms for the industry of repairing windmills, carried on by one of the last firms of millwrights in East Anglia, continued in Acle until recent times.

HORSEY MILL is a typical Norfolk drainage mill and is about fifteen miles along winding roads north-east from Norwich. You can reach it more directly however, from Great Yarmouth or Caister-on-Sea if you are visiting that area. Horsey Mill belongs to the National Trust and though it doesn't work now, all the machinery remains intact - in fact the present brick structure was built on the foundations of a much older wooden mill. The view from the balcony over the mere is wild, reed-hushed and bird-haunted, for Horsey stands where the marshy Broads approach the North Sea to within a mile or so. This is where there were devestating floods in 1938 and a huge barrier, over four miles of it, has now been built so that hopefully such a thing doesn't happen again.

SUTTON WINDMILL, not far from Horsey - about one mile off the A149 road from Caister - is Britain's tallest windmill. It was built in 1789 and its nine floors, extensively restored, are open for all to see. The display of milling machinery makes Sutton Mill one of the most handsome examples of a corn mill in these parts, and in the museum of the Broads attached you will find domestic tools, and other fascinating bygones by which you can trace the past of this country area. After you have descended from the panoramic viewing gallery you can then refresh yourself with coffee, tea and luxury ice-cream at the Broads Tearoom.

HUNSETT MILL, a mile or so north of Sutton and pretty as a post-card picture, is privately owned, so you can only sail by and admire its white-sailed, ivy-clad charm and picturesque riverside garden, framed with trees.

You can climb the nine floors of Sutton Mill and look out over Broadland. A Broads Museum now offers an additional reason for visiting.

At **HERRINGFLEET**, about ten miles south-west of Great Yarmouth on the River Waveney, you will find an old smock mill, still in working order. The mill has been preserved as an example of the many drainage mills which once pumped water from the low marshland into the enclosed Broads country before it was done by oil and electricity.

TAKING THE CHILDREN TOO . . .

In this area the Youth Hostels Association occasionally organises boat tours of both private and Norfolk Trust mills and pumps for their members.

Twenty-five miles north of Norwich on the B1149 the white-capped windmill near the quayside custom house at **CLEY-NEXT-THE-SEA** is a fine example of a brick-built tower mill. It was used for grinding corn until 1908 and though it has now been restored it is no longer working. It's now a private residence, but you can still climb its five floors and enjoy the superb view of the village with its great church beside a wide green, its pub and its harbour, all quaintly reminiscent of a Dutch landscape. The mill is also an arresting landmark through the cornfields or across the saltings on your way to or from the bird sanctuary at Cley Marshes. In fact it's now possible to stay at the mill, in one of three holiday cottages created from the stables and boat-sheds, and share some rooms in the mill itself.

GREAT BIRCHAM MILL, about thirty miles north-west of Norwich, is Norfolk's finest example of a corn mill. It stands in cornfields used for windmilling since the 1700s. Five floors up you can inspect all the milling machinery, now in working order. There's a bakery museum, gift shop, tea room and superb views over the Norfolk landscape, so a visit offers plenty of variety - enough to please even the most technically-minded, or the hungriest!

Two mills in remote and tiny places are **BILLINGFORD**, about twenty miles south of Norwich on the A143, one mile from east Scole, and **WICKLEWOOD MILL**, near Wymondham, about ten miles south-west of Norwich. The first is a fine example of a tower mill situated along the wide-watered Waveney valley. The mill was built in 1860 and is still working. It's open all year round and keys are available at the Horseshoes pub. The second is a five-storey tower mill containing much of the original machinery. It's also open all year round. Ask locally for the key.

BERNEY ARMS MILL Open 1 April-30 September daily, 9.30a.m.-6.30p.m.

STRACEY ARMS WINDPUMP Open 1 April-25 October daily, 9a.m.-8p.m.

HORSEY MILL Open during normal daylight hours, 20 April-30 September.

SUTTON WINDMILL Open 1 April-14 May daily, 1.30p.m.-6p.m., 15 May-30 Sept. 9.30a.m.-6p.m.

CLEY WINDMILL Open Whitsun - end September every day, 2-5p.m.

GREAT BIRCHAM MILL Open 7 April-19 May, Sunday, Wednesday and Bank Holidays; 20 May-end September daily (except Saturday) 10a.m.-5.30p.m.

BILLINGFORD WINDMILL Open all year, keys available at Horseshoes pub or by appointment with Norfolk Windmill Trust.

WICKLEWOOD MILL Open all year. Local keyholder.

STEAM ENGINES — AND SIMILAR DELIGHTS

Because so many branch railways are disappearing in this part of England which once bloomed with them, rides along meadowy tracks on miniature railway and antique steam locomotives lovingly refurbished by groups of volunteers have a unique nostalgia. To children who may never have experienced the countryside from such an angle they are a source of unending delight. So a day spent exploring one or two of these should appeal to everyone, whether they're true train buffs or have just come along for the ride.

To reach some mentioned here you need a car. Others are only a short train or bus ride from Norwich, and you could take a picnic or spend just half a day there if you felt like it.

Wells-next-the-Sea, where you will find the **WELLS AND WALSINGHAM LIGHT RAILWAY** is about your comfortable limit from Norwich in a day. In fact it's really worth staying at the resort itself for a night or so in order to savour its charming if slightly raffish atmosphere - more about which in a later chapter.

There's a strong stream of individuality coursing through the veins of many of the men of Norfolk. They have enough guts to do their own thing and to hell with what anybody else thinks, and very often they can make their own dreams come true. So it's not surprising that this railway turns out to be the realisation of one such dream - that of Lieutenant Commander R.W.Francis R.N., who after he retired spent thirteen years boat-building before he was able to attain his life's ambition: to build his own little railway on a strip of land he had spotted from the air, alongside the track bed of the 1857 Wells-Fakenham railway, long dismantled by British Rail.

Today the railway is the longest 10 inch gauge railway in Britain, and Lieutenant Commander Francis, who has spent most of his working life at sea, now passes most of his nights in a small but cosy caravan with all mod.cons., alongside his child - his beautiful green and copper engine and his red-painted carriages, which he runs from Easter to September with the help of one paid assistant, plus a band of volunteers.

But make no mistake - the Wells and Walsingham Light Railway isn't a toy. It is a proper light railway which is licensed by the government. For the technically-minded it's an example of brilliant engineering by an individualist. For other it is simply a magical four-mile ride that dips and climbs, displaying panoramic views of sand dune, sky and water, through a land of butterflies and brambly hedges, tall grasses and a glory of wild flowers.

Communication between guard and driver is by a system of electric bells, and stopping en route for the villagers at Warren and Wighton, you continue upwards over rolling meadows until you reach Walsingham, by far the prettiest way of making the most of a visit to that hallowed place.

During the height of the season Commander Francis organises two hour excursions to Walsingham, leaving time to wander round and have a meal before returning in the dark, lit by the glow of the engine.

Plans are now afoot to build a more powerful locomotive which could carry more passengers and would be longer than anything previously envisaged on a 10 gauge. Probably by the time you read this it will be finished, if enough money can be raised!

The **WELLS HARBOUR STEAM RAILWAY** was also built by Roy Francis. It has been sold, but in the holiday season this neat little track conveys visitors at regular intervals between the western end of Wells quay to the beach where the caravans are, a distance of about one mile. This is also where surf-boarding goes on and is a much more diverting way of getting there than by road.

THURSFORD, a small village not far from Wells off the A148 Fakenham-Holt road has become the centrepiece of the fulfilment of another man's dream. Over the years, owner George Cushing rescued dozens of elderly steam road locomotives, literally off the scrap heap, together with showmen's traction engines, ploughing and barn engines. He has lovingly restored them, and today, in a huge barn in the middle of an attractive small pleasure park set among pines he has transformed the lot into a collection which is said to be the world's biggest. Not only that, George has set his engines among some of the largest and rarest street and fairground organs in the world! Not such a disparate group of bedfellows as one might at first imagine.

Even if you're not technically minded, you will be thrilled by the sight of the magnificent engines poised cheek by jowl in all their burnished glory, awaiting the whistle that never comes. Around them stand an array of Dutch street organs and enormous mechanical fairground organs decorated with green, white and sugar-pink culicews, naked ladies and pastoral scenes, their golden pipes towering above. Some play music suddenly and spookily, their keys going up and down all by themselves. Others like the Mighty Wurlitzer, its 1339 pipes hidden behind huge doors, is one of the instruments performed on in daily recitals. At these everyone can join in their favourite choruses. Videos display in detail the organist's flying fingers and all the special effects, while Disney-like creatures descend from the ceiling from time to time and conduct the music. Dominating this whole extraordinary spectacle is Aspland's "Switchback" Roundabout. Here you can ride in one of the gold and red plush Royal Venetian Gondolas to the haunting music of an original Gavidi fairground organ.

For children it's a picture-book fairground come to life. For you - a slice of nostalgia, so flamboyant that the impact is almost physical. In fact the effect is so fantastic that it's difficult to realise that all the Thursford exhibits, engines as well as fairground objects, actually existed and gave pleasure to millions in their day. For serious organ experts, suffice it to say that the collection also includes a 112 keyless Carl Frei concert organ and another built in Antwerp in 1910 which has been altered to George Cushing's specifications, together with more than one turn-of-the-century Dutch organ. And the collection is being added to all the time.

Outside the Thursford Collection, in the pleasure park attached, there are switchbacks and other fun-things for the littler ones to play on, as well as plenty of space to picnic if you so wish. And the Thursford Steam Railway puffs its way through the woods from April to September.

You can obtain a Thursford leaflet from any local tourist office.

BRESSINGHAM GARDENS (which incorporate a live steam museum and railway rides) is 2½ miles west of Diss on the Norfolk-Suffolk border, in a direct line from Norwich. It's the creation of aptly named Alan Bloom, yet another living example of the East Anglian's independence and sense of purpose, for he has designed and planted these now internationally famous gardens himself over a period of thiry years.

Mr.Bloom is, however, also a collector and restorer of steam-engines, so you can combine a family visit to this plantly paradise with narrow-gauge rides through six acres of flowers, the sight of over fifty steam engines of various types, footplate journeys on main-line engines and trips on a real steam-driven roundabout with all the legendary fairground creatures on which to ride.

Barton House railway – a delight down by the Broads – check carefully for opening times. Sometimes you'll find wherries moored at the riverbank by the railway.

The **NORTH NORFOLK RAILWAY** is East Anglia's steam railway by the sea.

Reached easily from Norwich either by bus or pay-train, it has its home in the former BR station at Sheringham, the present one having obligingly moved about two hundred yards up the road.

The railway, which now puffs its way through beautiful countryside the three miles to Weybourne was originally part of the Midland and Great Northern Railway, most of it closed down as part of BR in 1959. This linked the Midlands with the North Norfolk coastal resorts. The line through to Mundesley was known affectionately as "The Poppy Line" and you will see why if you take this lovely ride in full summer.

With the help of an enthusiastic band of volunteers, plus David Madden - full time general manager and relief driver - and one full-time engineer, the line is being extended over Kelling Heath and eventually to Holt.

At Sheringham Station where the trains start there is a real old-fashioned buffet car undergoing restoration. You can visit the signal box and look at the old steam and early diesel locomotives, and on platform 1, next to the souvenir shop in the former booking hall there's an automatic model railway which you can work yourself. But behave because you are watched over by a severe life-sized guard in a glass case.

Each child who travels on the old steam train to Weybourne is given a leaflet before setting out with questions to answer, objects to spot and things to read about on the way, which makes the trip even more enjoyable. The ride passes between wood and heathland on one hand, and on the other past meadows which tone from delicate green and yellow to palest blue, as you open to panoramic views of the sea beyond the golf links. At Weybourne, a typical country station of the 1900s you alight, have a cup of (real) coffee, buy a railway souvenir from the tiny shop on the platform if you wish, and look around the works where steam locomotives are being restored and refurbished, like the old Peckett engine. The actual workshops are normally closed to the public but if you ask permission it's sometimes possible for small groups to be taken round. And anyway you will have a good view of much of it from the station platform. Weybourne station has featured in several films and TV series, among them BBC TV's "Hi-di-Hi" and "Poppyland" - a Victorian drama - and also "Miss Marple".

BARTON HOUSE RAILWAY is only eight miles north of Norwich on the A1151, or a short rail ride to Wroxham, shopping centre and cheerful little hub of Broadland. It offers a $3\frac{1}{2}''$ gauge miniature steam railway, as well as a $7\frac{1}{4}''$ gauge track that skirts the river. You can go on train rides on the third Sunday of each month from April to October - if you can work all that out beforehand!

WELLS AND WALSINGHAM LIGHT RAILWAY Open Good Friday-30th September daily. First trains from Wells, 10a.m. Evening trips on Wednesdays in July and August.

THURSFORD COLLECTION Open 28th March-31st October daily 2-5.30p.m. March and November, Sundays 2-5p.m. Closed January, February. Special Christmas events only during December.

BRESSINGHAM LIVE STEAM MUSEUM AND GARDENS Open Easter, 19,20 April, Sundays 26 April-27 September. Thursdays, 4 June-10 September. Wednesdays in August only. Bank holidays in May and August.

NORTH NORFOLK RAILWAY 28 March-28 September daily. October-Easter Saturday and Sunday 10a.m.-5p.m. Steam trains Sheringham-Weybourne every Sunday, and other advertised days in summer.

BARTON HOUSE RAILWAY Train rides April-October 3rd Sunday in each month. Easter Monday 2.30-5.30p.m.

ANIMALS WITHOUT TEARS

Wildlife and aviary parks where animals and birds are reasonably free to wander about and enjoy life need rather less soul-searching as places of entertainment, perhaps, than do zoos. And the wide stretches of meadow, wood and marshland in North and East Norfolk seem more suited to the dignity and space in which such creatures should exist (if indeed we must incarcerate wild animals at all) than others in more restricted areas of England.

There are tiny spots like **PETTITTS**, just outside Reedham, a short train ride from Norwich, where you can wander in small and pleasant gardens among pheasants, ornamental ducks and other attractive wildfowl. Here, small children can pet and feed tame animals such as goats and donkeys and have rides on very small ponies. This is a diverting pastime for toddlers on sunny days, especially as there are good picnic areas at Pettitts, which itself has a refreshment booth for soft drinks and ices, together with an adventure playground and massive snake slide extension!

At the other extreme the **NORFOLK WILDLIFE PARK** at Great Witchingham - a twelve mile bus ride from the centre of Norwich (buses stop outside the park) claims to have the largest collection of British and European mammals in the world, from Barbary Apes to Reindeer. Families who care about conservation and wildlife will be pleased to know that a speciality is made of breeding endangered species like eagles, otters, badgers and coypu and the animals are exhibited in semi-natural enclosures among more that forty acres of parkland. There are wild fowl lakes and walk-through aviaries and especially for children a Model Farm and Pets' Corner where some of the animals can be fed and stroked. There are two adventure play areas and the children will also enjoy the special play equipment which has been newly constructed.

On Saturdays two children per adult are admitted free. There are picnic areas, souvenir shops and a tea-room and the Park is open all year round from 10-30a.m. until sunset.

Six miles north of Norwich, off the B1150, the **REDWINGS HORSE SANCTUARY** offers rescued horses and ponies a break from a life-time's drudgery and a happy home for the rest of their life. You can talk to them and spoil them a bit with lumps of sugar in their stall and also have pony rides. The Sanctuary is open from the beginning of April until the end of October on Sunday afternoons, but if you want to take a party you can arrange an appointment for any other time.

Further north still, in fact as far as you are likely to go for a comfortable day out you will find the two hundred acres of the **SALTHOUSE** and **CLEY MARSHES** controlled by the Norfolk Naturalists' Trust. In 1966 Cley Marshes became an official bird sanctuary under the Protection of Birds Act, and on each arm of these silent shingly stretches nearly three hundred species of birds have been recorded: some rare - others the more homely swans, ducks and Brent geese. Some are winter visiting, others resting briefly on their journeys to warmer resorts, and others actually breeding there. You can watch them from an observation hut or hides on the marsh, but you need a permit first which is easily obtained nearby, unless you are already a member of the Trust.

A mile or so south-east of Cley the **KELLING PARK AVIARY** at Kelling Heath, specially beautiful in heathery late summer and autumn, includes tropical birds like cockatoos, parrots, ostriches, sunset-pink flamingoes and long-legged cranes among its treats. The Aviary is at Holt, and if you're going to either Cromer or Sheringham for the day, it's well worth making a short detour to pay it a visit, because Holt itself is a delightful small market town with its wide streets, attractive book and craft centres. It is also the home of Greshams, the school where composer Benjamin Britten was educated. At the Aviaries there is both a cafeteria and a restaurant, as well as a pottery and gift shop - so everyone will have a diverting time there. The Aviary may soon be reached by way of the North Norfolk Railway direct from Sheringham.

Also in the Sheringham-Cromer area is the **NORFOLK SHIRE HORSE CENTRE** where children can make friends with some of the Shire, Suffolk and Clydesdale horses who have come there for a little holiday before returning to work for some of the big breweries.

Twice daily there is the chance to attend harnessing and working demonstrations and talks. There are videos of working horses and a permanent collection of horse-drawn machinery, wagons and carts on exhibition. Little mountain and moorland ponies also live at the Centre, neatly penned in their green pastures like horses on a toy farm, and you'll have an opportunity to see

The Shire Horse Centre is very much a centre of activity – you can ride like these young visitors, watch the horses being groomed or see horse drawn ploughs in action.

The reindeer stars of the film Santa Claus – The Movie now live in Philip Wayre's Norfolk Wildlife Park at Great Witchingham. You probably won't visit when there's snow on the ground, but it does give them a chance to show their skill at pulling a sleigh.

some of their foals if you come at the right time. Take a picnic - there's plenty of space in the grounds - or buy refreshments on the spot.

Visiting the Shire Horse Centre will assist in the recovery of the heavy horse returning to both agriculture and commerce, for a breeding programme is being undertaken, so that these powerful, gentle giants can be brought back into service.

The Centre is also the home for **WEST RUNTON STABLES**, where the more equestrian youngsters - beginners or expert riders - may enjoy accompanied rides, through tracks between the unspoiled countryside and the sea. There's a special covered all-weather riding school where you can take basic riding lessons by the hour, but the owners also arrange riding holidays for unaccompained children and teenagers.

HICKLING is the largest of the Norfolk Broads and one of Norfolk's widest stretches of water - three miles in circumference. On the Broad itself, the Norfolk Naturalist's Trust has put up observation hides, and the Broad contains some enormous pike. Sometimes the Youth Hostels Association organises boat tours of the Nature Reserve, so it's very well worth while belonging as a family before you set off on holiday to these parts, in case you are able to join in.

About twelve miles north-east of Norwich (quite near Great Yarmouth in fact, between Caister and Acle) the **THRIGBY HALL WILDLIFE GARDENS**, open all the year round from 10a.m. until dusk, have an exciting collection of Asian mammals, birds and reptiles. There's a waterfowl lake, aviaries and tarzan nets too, all set in the 250 year old landscaped grounds and gardens of Thrigby Hall. If it rains you can spend fascinating hours in the tropical and bird houses, or in the theatre-ette, where there are free slide shows. The Wildlife Gardens have a children's play area, and a cafe to give everyone time to re-charge their batteries for a day in the open air.

Out of Norfolk, but only about twenty miles south-east of Norwich the **OTTER TRUST** at Earsham, near Bungay (irresistible in its own right - don't miss it!), has a large collection of otters from all over the world. The Trust is a public charity devoted to the conservation of those engaging animals and the grounds, with riverside walks, three lakes and a spectacular collection of waterfowl are set in the lovely surroundings of the Waveney Valley with large and semi-natural enclosures and a stream flowing through each enclosure - most important for the inhabitants.

The idea is that the breeding centre should release enough young animals into the wild each year to save the otter from extinction, and since three cubs bred at the Trust were released in July 1983 it is becoming an annual event. Proceeds go to otter conservation and research, so a visit to the Centre ensures that you are further supporting the environment.

Five miles south of Lowestoft - again in Suffolk - the **SUFFOLK WILDLIFE AND COUNTRY PARK** at Kessingland has a large array of animals, birds and reptiles and in the afternoons you may be able to watch up-to-date milking methods in the sparkling new milking parlour. Zebras, deer, emus and monkeys enjoy a peaceful existence among woodland marshes and a large area of grassland and in the Pet's Corner, the youngest visitor can spend a happy and loving time amongst the furry and tame animals.

PETTITTS OF REEDHAM Camp Hill, Reedham. Open Easter - end October, Monday-Friday 10a.m.-6p.m. Sunday 1p.m.-5.30p.m. Closed Saturday.

NORFOLK WILDLIFE PARK Great Witchingham. Open daily, all year. 10a.m.-6p.m. (or sunset)

REDWINGS HORSE SANCTUARY Hall Lane, Frettenham. Open 7th April-end October. Sunday 2-4.30p.m. Parties at any time by appointment.

CLEY VISITOR CENTRE (for **CLEY MARSHES**) Permits for Nature Reserve obtainable from here. Open April-October, Tuesday-Sunday. 10a.m.-5p.m.

KELLING PARK AVIARIES Weybourne Road, Holt. Open all year round, daily 10a.m.-8p.m.

NORFOLK SHIRE HORSE CENTRE West Runton. Open Easter until end September. Daily, 10a.m.-5p.m, closed Saturday.

HICKLING BROAD Warden's office: Stubb Road, Hickling. Open 9-10a.m. and 1-2p.m. for permits. Water trail 2 hour trip in boat, June-mid September, Tuesday, Wednesday, Thursday.

THRIGBY HALL WILDLIFE GARDENS near Filby, Great Yarmouth. Open all year, daily, 10a.m.-5p.m. or dusk. Gift shop in Hall, Whitsun-October.

OTTER TRUST Earsham, near Bungay, Suffolk. Open 1st April-31st October, daily, 10.30a.m.-5.30p.m. or dusk.

SUFFOLK WILDLIFE AND COUNTRY PARK Kessingland, near Lowestoft. Open Easter to end October, 10a.m.-6p.m. or 1 hour before dusk. (Dates liable to change)

CRAFTSMEN AT WORK

One of the most absorbing things to do, especially if the weather isn't all that bright, is to watch other people making things.

There's no dearth of working-craftsmen in East Anglia. The only problem is deciding which ones to visit. Many encourage visitors to their studios, and there's no doubt that a pot or a wooden toy or a piece of glowing material is doubly precious if you have been close to the love and care that gave it birth.

Some craft centres even organise special workshops for children who can then come away with objects they have actually made themselves, but these generally require advance booking.

WROXHAM BARNS, set in grassy meadowland, is only one mile from Wroxham, bright and busy little "gateway to Broadland" - itself only a twenty minute ride from Norwich on the pay-train. They comprise a collection of eighteenth century barns where visitors are welcome to watch resident artists and craftsmen at work spinning, turning wood, glass-engraving, lace-making and so on. Star turn is perhaps the boat-buildings sheds where steam launches are restored and traditional craft are built with the help of new steam and electrical techniques. You could easily spend an entertaining half day there, having passed the other half enjoying a taste of life on the Broads, as recommended on page 39. You can also buy hand made shawls and babies' and children's clothes, quilted carry-cots, lots of toys (hand-made and otherwise) and other seductive things in the roomy craft-galleries, or order something to be made specifically for you.

Picnic in freedom in the surrounding grasslands where there's also a small playground with swings. Talk to the horses, or consume delicious light lunches and teas under the fine beamed roof of one of the caringly restored barns. On certain weekends outdoor field attractions are also arranged.

At the **FEATHERCRAFT WORKSHOPS** a short walk from pretty riverside Reedham, which you can very quickly reach from Norwich on the Yarmouth pay-train, you can watch the local ladies creating magnificent bridal bouquets, buttonholes, table decorations and even pictures all from dyed turkey and goose feathers, which are then supplied to shops throughout the country. Outside the workshops which are set in charming landscape, visitors can stroll around and admire peacocks, pheasants and beautiful waterfowl of all kinds, and can picnic in the surrounding meadows - all part of the Pettitts enterprise.

NORWICH itself caters generously for the brass-rubbing fraternity at the Brass Rubbing Centre in St.Peter Hungate, at the top of cobbled Elm Hill.

Materials are supplied and a wide selection of facsimile brasses are available from which to work. Entrance is free, but there is a scale of charges for doing the rubbing.

In nearby St.Andrew's Street there's always a Saturday crafts market in St.Andrew's Hall where local crafts people offer their own work for sale. On any Saturday you might find brightly-coloured wooden toys and household objects, hand-sewn children's garments that you're unlikely to see elsewhere, cloth dolls of distinct personality, original and funny badges and brooches for teenagers, and some finely worked jewellery for special occasions. In fact the charm of these East Anglian crafts markets, of which St.Andrews is a high class example, is that no item is ever exactly the same, so you can be pretty sure of coming away with something with lots of character.

There's usually a stall selling home-made sweets and other goodies, and always fresh coffee and snacks in the Crypt Coffee Bar, which you can consume peacefully among the cloisters in a sort of glassed-in garden.

At Erpingham, about fifteen miles from Cromer on the A140 between Cromer and Aylsham, is **ALBY CRAFTS**, a superbly restored group of Norfolk farm buildings set in lawns and gardens. Here you will find galleries selling hundreds of items made by British craftsmen, and a collection of studio shops housing young artists, some of whom live on the complex. You can spend time with them as they create a variety of beautiful things from toys to silk-screen prints, for the exhibitions are constantly changing. There is a fascinating lace museum too, and Alby Crafts is also a very good place for everyone to have tea.

About seven miles from the centre of Great Yarmouth an exciting new project is due to open in May 1987. This is **BURGH HALL BYGONE VILLAGE** at Fleggburgh, where a complete 19th century village has been brought to life. Once within its boundaries you enter a world of the 1800s. There's a wooded estate with a working saw-mill, a farm, and cottages inside which the visitor can watch the crafts of yesteryear. A steam passenger train will take everyone on lakeside excursions, and on the farm there are animals which the littler visitor can see and touch.

WELLS-NEXT-THE-SEA, a sprightly little port-cum-seaside resort with pebble and flint cottages which look impervious to the biting north wind. A visit to the Wells Art Centre in Staithe Street will provide the whole family with plenty of diversion and occupation, as well as offering the chance to sit down and enjoy a variety of delicious home-cooked nourishing snacks and good coffee.

The Centre was started off by actor Michael Gough, so it has a strong tradition of theatrical attractions of all kinds. Now run under new direction that tradition is carried on with a lot for children to join in and enjoy. Activities for them are generally geared to the school holidays, but in term time there is often an artist in residence who organises regular classes and workshops. If you book ahead you can take part in these, otherwise, anyone can wander in and watch. At different times you will discover painting, sculpture, dance, mime, clowns, magic and juggling going on as well as the Norfolk Children's Theatre

It's quite impossible to predict the variety of activities at the Wells Centre, so call ahead for a copy of their brochure. Here sculptor Claire Guest is leading a 'Making Waves' project.

Company. The best thing to do, once you're sure you'll be in the vicinity is to write in advance for a programme, so you know exactly what's being offered at the time you plan to be there.

For grown-ups the Wells Centre presents concerts and recitals by some of the best young musicians in the country, sometimes making their debut. It also offers excellent repertory theatre, jazz, poetry and many of the best films of the year.

THOM BORTHWICK used to run the pottery studio at nearby Holkham Hall. Now he has his own little one on the outskirts of Wells where visitors are welcome to stroll around and watch him at work - providing they're careful not to knock over the pots in various stages of completion all over the place! These you can buy at very reasonable prices, as well as some engaging little figures and animals, and Thom and his wife also sell pot-pourri gathered from their own garden.

LANGHAM is only a short distance from Wells; in fact if you were feeling really energetic you could probably walk it. Recently the whole village has been open to the public on one summer's day a year. Teas are served from cottage gardens, produce is sold and everyone is welcome to enjoy the community goings-on. A delightful idea which, hopefully, may spread to other pretty villages in East Anglia - if it hasn't done so already.

The fascination of glass being pulled, twisted and blown into shape is found at Langham Glass House.

In a large flinty barn at Langham a team of glass-makers are to be found at work blowing the treacly glass and fashioning it with red-hot irons into goblets, paper-weights and miniature animals with an ease that comes with absolute confidence and dexterity. You can watch it all from a special viewing area in the workshop gallery, and in order to continue this age-old craft the Master Glass-Maker is already beginning to train some local youngsters to carry on the tradition. All the glass made here, and also other highly presentable glass objects, is on sale in the Gift Shop, and after you've had a good look round you can relax and consume tea with home-made cakes and scones and locally cured ham in the attractive tea-room attached.

BURGH HALL Bygone village, Fleggburgh. Opening May 3, 10a.m.-6p.m. daily.

WROXHAM BARNS Open every day 10a.m.-6p.m.

PETTITTS of Reedham - **FEATHERCRAFT** Open Easter - end October Monday-Friday 10a.m.-6p.m.,Sundays 1-5.30p.m.

ST.ANDREW'S HALL Norwich Saturday Craft Market 10a.m.-5p.m.

ALBY CRAFTS Open 10a.m.-5p.m. Closed Monday, 11th March-14th December

WELLS-NEXT-THE-SEA Arts Centre. Write for programme to: The Wells Centre, Staithe Street, Wells-next-the-Sea, Norfolk NR23 1AN

LANGHAM GLASS HOUSE Glass making Monday to Friday, January-December. Also Sundays at Bank Holiday weekends and in June to October.

BEACHES, BOATS . . .

The beaches within easy reach of Norwich are many and varied. Too many to mention more than a few personal favourites here, for they range from fun-places pure and simple, through golden stretches of sand perfect for riding, castle-building and exhilarating walks, to quaint little ports and wild expanses of silent coastline where you might be poised at the edge of the world.

All round the north and east Norfolk coast the north-easterly wind, combined with the sunshine, makes you feel as clean and sharp as a whistle right through. You absorb energy with every breath as though you had just consumed some invigorating spa-water.

GREAT YARMOUTH is only a short train ride from Norwich, and a pretty one. Here you'll find all the fun of the fair and endless entertainment for children: ice-lollies and bubble-gum all day if you wish. You can pick from a tantalising mix of Punch and Judy, trampolines and inflatable castles, a boating lake and supervised activities at the children's play-area by Marine Parade and the kalaiedoscope of attractions it has to offer.

However - there's another Great Yarmouth with quite a different fascination for children (as well as grown-ups) as you'll discover if you take an alternative route into the town and turn to page 11.

If you're based in Norwich and without a car, remember to find out from the railway or bus timetable about any money-saving travel tickets which are available, such as the "go anywhere in a day" ones. At the time of writing, about £7.50 (child 5-15 year; £4) gives you a day's unlimited rail travel to all the best places around East Anglia, and certainly a pleasant ride by either bus or train will take you quite quickly to either **CROMER** or **SHERINGHAM** where there are lovely beaches. Both resorts retain echoes of those times when monstrous old ladies in bath chairs were wheeled along the prom by brow-beaten companions, and nursemaids in streamered caps hustled their small charges down to the beach like sheepdogs.

CROMER's beaches shelve down gently from the high cliffs, and from the pier, at the end of which is the town's famous lifeboat, you can watch the tide gently lapping, deckle-edged like lace, leaving expanses of golden sand where there's enormous scope for castle building.

The town is bright and jolly and there's plenty laid of for children, like a boating lake and dodger cars and yet the place retains its old world atmosphere. The streets of the old to n, flanked with tall houses, shops, pubs and whelk and shrimp stalls, are as curled about as the whelk and winkle shells themselves, and on the beach the prettily painted fishing boats perch on the shingle waiting to go to work.

For sheer magic, however, and a place not to be missed, is **CROMER MUSEUM,** for it is probably one of the most charming of its kind in Norfolk. Run by the Norfolk Museums Service and in the charge of young and enthusiastic curator Martin Warren it is situated in a row of Victorian fishermen's cottages snuggled in the lee of the church. Outside is a yard with a pump, wash-house and a tiny garden with a wooden fence. Inside there's a surprise round every corner. On the ground floor you have the story of the fisherman's trade: his clothes and crab-pots, photographs of crews and heroic rescues. But most engaging is the full size replica of the fisherman's home depicted in every detail. In fact you just stop yourself saying 'Hello!' as you pass through his kitchen with its gas lamps and family portraits and laundry drying on the range where he sits relaxing, while his wife mixes pastry at the table, recipe book in hand. Upstairs are the austere little bedrooms with their brass bedsteads, white counterpanes and tracts on the walls. You'll see odd clothes and books lying about, and in the main bedroom there's a fold-down chest-bed, surprisingly modern in conception, yet typical of the period. Altogether a scene of simple Victorian cottage life made vividly real.

You're unlikely to see Cromer Lifeboat and the lifeboat house from this angle, but the boathouse and the lifeboat museum are a must for a visit. To catch the lifeboats in action – frequently with a helicopter in attendance – look out for posters for Lifeboat Days at Great Yarmouth, Caister, Sea Palling, Hemsby, Happisburgh, Mundesley, Cromer, Sheringham and Wells.

At every twist and turn of the landings you'll find exhibits depicting the birds, beasts, shells and habitat of the region and for two days each summer there's usually an exhibition of the making of traditional crab pots, given in the yard by a retired lifeboat coxswain.

As a bonus an excellent child-orientated brochure is to be had in the Museum which contains easily understood notes and pictures about fish and fishermen, crabs and shannocks, and a big picture to colour.

A word or two here about 'Poppyland' - examples of which are to be found in the museum. The name is evocative of those flowers which make the hedgerows and cornfields bright from Sheringham to Mundesley and was given to the area by one Clement Scott, a journalist of the 1880s. So seductive were his articles about this part of the country which appeared in 'The Daily Telegraph' of those times that people flocked there in their thousands and 'Poppyland' became a household name. All sorts of 'poppy' souvenirs evolved: poppy decorated china, poppy jam-pots, poppy postcards and even a perfume. You'll see some of these in the Museum, souvenirs which today are much sought after and extremely pretty if you are lucky enough to find any in a junk shop.

In **CROMER LIFEBOAT MUSEUM** there are lots of exhibits which give a graphic picture of what the lifeboat service is about, with relics of vessels washed ashore, models of lifeboats, real used lifebelts, and pictures of rescues -while the new Cromer Lifeboat "Ruby and Arthur Reed 11" stands at the ready, twenty-four hours a day at the end of the pier.

SHERINGHAM, a bit further west along the coast, has a gently sloping sandy beach at low tide. Small children with buckets can poke and potter and search for fishy treasures among the shallow pools left behind. At both resorts you can enjoy scrumptious fresh-caught crab teas, as well as other local fish, and though there's no lack of places to eat, from fast-food to four course meals, both Cromer and Sheringham leave you more to your own devices to watch seabirds, the crab boats, to swim, paddle and enjoy a sense of freedom than, say, the Alladin's Caves of Great Yarmouth or Wells-next-the-Sea.

When you get off the train at Sheringham you experience a sense of order and "lightness", a certain gentility which one connects more with a resort of the 1920's than of today. The few amusement arcades, as well as the old fashioned Joke Shop, appear to be tucked tidily in one corner of the town, but the rows of fishermen's cottages, some with crab pots set ready at the foot of neat front gardens, trickle in rows towards the cliff tops overlooking the lovely sandy beach. The upper beach is very stoney, and at high tide all the sand is hidden, but the compensation is the glorious expanse of sand when the tide is out.

Old folk sit quietly on the cliff tops or in the seaside gardens sheltered from the North Sea breezes enjoying the sunshine. But children love the wide sandy beaches; and on the west cliff top it's also possible to go pony-riding. Also at the west end of the promenade is another major attraction; the lifeboat station run by the R.N.L.I. Here, shining with new paint, the Sheringham Lifeboat stands waiting, with a platform alongside so that visitors can inspect it both from above and below.

Around the walls are plaques from way back to the present day commemorating dates when the lifeboats were called out, and to what events. The lists of rescues include many crab boats and other fishing vessels; there are boat-type souvenirs to buy, ranging from tee-shirts to postcards, so no-one need come away empty handed (or empty-pocketed for that matter - they're mostly quite cheap!)

At the other end of the prom you'll find the red, white and blue fishing boats lined up on the slipway ready to go crab or lobster catching, and above, now at rest in a shed of its own, you will find the **HENRY RAMEY UPCHER** lifeboat and equipment which was launched in 1892; she is one of the last rowing and sailing lifeboats in existence. The museum is open two or three days a week (which vary) and entrance is free.

Sheringham's British Rail station has moved up the road and at its old abode you will find the home of the North Norfolk Railway with its tiny museum, from where you can chuff along on a shining old steam engine the three panoramic miles to pretty little Weybourne. But you can read all about that in an earlier chapter.

WELLS-NEXT-THE-SEA is about the farthest from Norwich that you can do comfortably on a day trip (better still, stay a day or so!) It's a cheerful and charming small port cum seaside resort, very crowded during the season so possibly more enjoyable in early spring and autumn.

Fishing and smuggling were once industries. Today, as well as being a popular holiday centre, it's an invigorating mix of working port harbouring Dutch vessels and other foreign coasters, attractive pebble and flint fishermen's cottages, narrow shopping streets, whelk sheds and amusement arcades.

You can spend all morning playing space invaders, and all afternoon sitting on the picturesque quayside watching the fishing boats land their catch of sprats, whelks and prawns, or trying to spot where all the foreign coasters have come from with their various cargoes. However Wells is not actually next-the-sea at all, for the pine fringed beach is about a mile from the port against sand dunes. You can reach it from the quay by road, but it's much more interesting to putter up and down on the little 10″ railway which does the trip several times a day during the season to help the caravanners do their shopping in the town.

Wells' beach is sandy and shingly, and nearby is the former harbour, now a boating lake with pine trees on one side called, charmingly, "Abraham's Bosom". Here you can go yachting, surfboarding and water ski-ing.

Wells is unique in that local youngsters are specially trained to become part of its group of volunteer life-guards who are always on duty in this sometimes treacherous sea area.

HOLKHAM beach is only a short drive from Wells - quite a different kettle of fish. This is a private beach reached along quiet Lady Anne's Drive opposite the lane to Holkham Village, and in summer you have to pay to park there.

It's a marvellous spot for picnicking because you are sheltered by pines and sand dunes. There's room and to spare to bring the dogs, fling your arms about, shout, swim and explore - or just quietly birdwatch under the Norfolk sky. A thoroughly releasing experience.

For a short trip from Norwich on a sunny day, however, you could take the pay-train from that city to **REEDHAM** - about a twenty minute ride.

Though tiny, there's plenty going on, for all sorts of craft, both working and playing, sail past Reedhams's waterside between Norwich and the sea.

The towpath with its attractive pubs and one or two small shops is the hub of the village. You could spend hours watching coasters from distant parts toting their loads between Great Yarmouth and Norwich, or looking into the microcosm of domestic life played out on the decks of holiday launches: toddlers in striped jerseys, screaming and red faced, teenagers in jeans and tee-shirts being competent with ropes and steering wheels...happy dogs out for the day mudlarking, shaking river water over passers-by. And there's a chain ferry which bears you romantically from the Ferry pub over the water into Suffolk - and that's a different world.

Nor should you miss visiting Pettitts (also mentioned in an earlier chapter) which is about a one mile walk, or a very short drive, from Reedham station away from the waterfront. Here in a miniature zoo are goats and sheep to pat and feed, ponies to ride and some beautiful ornamental birds to wander among. Plenty of grassy picniking spots too, plus light refreshments on sale.

Pettitts also do a big trade in hiring out stuffed animal heads to theatre companies, and in the Trophy House you will find an awesome collection of these, including a stuffed python - whole!

The **NORFOLK BROADS** of which Reedham is a part, are a subject (and a holiday) that deserve a book to themselves, and anyway much has already been written about them. However, a taste of their subtle enchantment is a must, especially as you can reach **WROXHAM** - heart of the Broads - in about twenty minutes on another pay-train which starts from Norwich and saunters through the countryside, sometimes paralleling the river, sometimes giving the impression you are travelling through the middle of cornfields.

Wroxham itself is a pleasant place. Busy, because it's the shopping centre for people holidaying on the Broads. Nevertheless the town has its own bright charm and is a first rate jumping-off ground for a short exploration by water. **BROADS TOURS** offer a choice of short or whole day boat excursions complete with commentary, light refreshments and a loo on board, so you can choose the tour that best suits the ages and interests of your brood.

One such, starting from Wroxham at 11a.m., takes two and a half hours. Past pretty bungalows you sail, where seagulls perch like sentinels on the rooftops, alongside woods and reedy banks busy with waterfowl of all kinds. In fact a diverting time could be spent on one of these trips counting how many different kinds of birds you can spot on the way.

Soon you spread out across the twenty acres of silvery Wroxham Broad when, if the yacht-racing's on, your boat weaves skilfully between the racing craft. On you go to Salhouse Broad, a picture book setting framed in woodland, with flowery meadows sloping down to water shallow enough for children to paddle.

A perfect place for a picnic on another sunny day, for Salhouse is only a stop along the pay-train line from Norwich - though Salhouse station is a walk away from Salhouse village and Broad.

Then to Horning whose village street trickles along with the river, and whose cottage gardens slope to the water's edge with tiny canals running up the sides.

As well as the fourteenth century cottage where Nelson is said to have spent time off you will pass every kind of holiday abode from tiny summer cabins to cool mansions. This is also the way to view at close range some of the attractive windmills in the area which are not open to the public, but have been converted to summertime homes, their bright gardens overlooking the river.

For serious nature lovers, Broads Tours can organise special water-borne Nature Trail tours on Wednesdays from 10th July to 4th September. These are whole day trips, and must be booked in advance.

Your skipper will be someone specially picked for his interest in the flora and fauna of the Broads, and at selected places there are guides who will tell you about the features you can expect to see. This whole area teems with birds, butterflies, waterfowl and the occasional small mammal. You might catch a fleeting glimpse of the swallowtail butterfly, hear a bittern boom, come across some of the rare marshland flowers. To anyone interested in nature and the conservation of the countryside this is a very special day out, and one that can be done easily and comfortably if you're staying in Norwich.

You start from Wroxham in the morning, alighting at Bure Marshes for a walk through part of the Bure Marshes National Nature Reserve. Then you continue to Ranworth Church which is one of the loveliest on the Broads. It has an extremely fine mediaeval rood screen and from the tower, which you can climb, you have a marvellous view of Broadland and the tree lined river banks. Lastly you pay a privileged visit to Cockshoot Broad. Privileged because this is a private Broad - a paradise for naturalists - which cannot be seen by ordinary visitors to these parts. You can bring your own lunch, or buy tea, coffee and crisps on board and you'll be furnished with an information pack full of fascinating things to read and look out for on your arrival. Be prepared with waterproof shoes and clothing. But whether it's fine or not, this is an unforgettable experience.

CROMER MUSEUM Open Monday 10a.m.-1p.m., 2-5p.m. Tuesday-Saturday 10a.m.-5p.m., Sunday 2-5p.m., closed Good Friday, 25th, 26th December.

CROMER LIFEBOAT MUSEUM Open 1st May-31st September daily 9a.m.-12.30p.m., 2-5p.m. (except in very bad weather)

HOLKHAM BEACH Open all year.

PETTITTS CRAFTS AND GARDENS Open Easter - end October, Monday-Friday 10a.m.-6p.m.,Sunday 1-5.30p.m., closed Saturday.

BROADS TOURS LIMITED Station Road, Wroxham, Norwich, Norfolk NR12 8UR

. . . AND BEING EXPLORERS

North Norfolk is a marvellous area for deserted heath and marshland suddenly silvered with little inlets and waterways guarding who knows what secrets and dramas over the years.

No one is too young to learn how to watch and listen: to be aware of stillness. The rewards are great, for what you find will call you back and back for a sort of spiritual refreshment over the rest of your life.

Tread with care in these parts. You may find plants you have never seen before. Stand still. For wild-life you may never have encountered at such close quarters may be shaded into the sepia of fallen leaves and branches and among the hushing reeds. If you listen you may discover a whole orchestra of birdsong in what you thought was silence.

For exploring such spots, the best and most accessible from Norwich is the coastline between Burnham Overy Staithe and Sheringham. Not only is it beautiful but it includes the largest coastal national nature reserve in Britain, much of it managed by the National Trust.

BURNHAM OVERY STAITHE is on the creek some way from the sea. It includes in the village, granaries and maltings and is a lovely quiet place from which to watch small-boat sailing. Lady Anne's Drive, mentioned in the last chapter as access from Wells to wild and private Holkham Beach and bay is also one way of getting to Overy Staithe along the sand-dunes and marshes protected by handsome Corsican pines. Another way is from the beach at Wells-next-the-Sea.

The National Trust isn't all gracious living. Its properties range from medieval abbeys and canal-side cottages to isolated dove cotes, and in North Norfolk the Trust owns miles of magical beaches and bird sanctuaries, such as **SCOLT HEAD ISLAND**, west of Overy Staithe - a major breeding ground for shore nesting birds. In summer you can be ferried to the nature reserve by local boatmen from nearby Brancaster Staithe, but it is not advisable to walk across the marshes to the Island unless you know the area very well. The reserve is a haunt of ducks and waders, and a breeding ground for oyster catchers, terns and other shore nesting birds and you may be able to spot some of the rare species of migrant birds - if you keep quiet and still.

BLAKENEY, a few miles east of Wells, is a neat mini-holiday resort, complete with hotels, pubs and a caravan site. There's a boat service which goes from Morston Quay to the Blakeney Point Nature Reserve, a lonely mix of saltings and sand-dunes which has been a reserve since 1912. Boats will also take you to see the seals off Blakeney Point and to wander over the great barrier island there. In the Lifeboat House at Blakeney Point there is a small shop run by the National Trust which sells special publications for young visitors, as well as postcards, sweets, soft drinks and some souvenirs.

In the horseshoe shaped Blakeney harbour there's safe bathing and paddling for children and plenty of opportunity for mud-larking among the saltings, while at **BRANCASTER STAITHE** all types of bicycles, including tandems and children's models can be hired by the week, day or half-day at Easter and from May to September. Enquire at the National Trust Information Centre on the Staithe.

For older teenagers the Trust runs two of its **ACORN CAMP SCHEMES** in this area, one on the Blickling Estate, near Aylsham, and one on the Felbrigg Estate, near Cromer.

You have to be at least seventeen to be eligible and enjoy working hard in beautiful and unspoiled spots. Lovers of the simple life (you'll be housed in a former coach-house in a stable block) and those who care strongly about conservation of the countryside will find this sort of short holiday especially attractive. Work could include helping to build new stiles and bridge, improving access footpaths and various tasks around woodlands and lakes.

It's a great way of getting to know the secrets of wild places in a degree of solitude, as the camps prefer people coming either on their own or with one other person. Best suited, therefore to boys and girls coming with a buddy, though there will be plenty of others with similar tastes on the camp itself.

At the time of writing there's a charge of £16.00 to help cover the cost of board and lodging.

In addition, and especially for youngsters, the enterprising National Trust organises Young National Trust Groups. These arrange social events, theatre trips and barbecues, plus twice-monthly Sunday work parties and regular weekends away, all doing interesting and varied conservation work for the Trust. This could include dry-stone walling, tree-planting or footpath maintenance and incidentally volunteers for either of these schemes don't have to be members of the Trust in order to take part. For details of both Acorn Camps and Young National Trust Groups in the Norwich area see the end of this chapter.

The quiet saltmarshes at **STIFFKEY**, east of Wells, painted the colours of sea-lavender and sea-aster, are the winter feeding-grounds for terns. There is a track and footpaths along the marshes' edges to **MORSTON MARSHES** from either Blakeney or Stiffkey.

In the marshland at **CLEY** a few miles further east you will find a large number of rare migrating birds. To explore you'll need a permit which is available at nearby Cley Visitor Centre, high up overlooking the marshes. Inside you will find conservation displays and a history of the area, together with a gift shop.

But there's much much more of magic and beauty in this land of hidden tracks, waterways and whispering marshes if you've a mind to find it. Even if you simply take the car, drive to some deserted spot and keep all your senses on the alert. And though it's possible to make your first exploration to these remote places a bit at a time, from Norwich, you also need space to live with them a little. Follow up your initial visits by finding somewhere nearby in Wells or Cley or Blakeney for bed-and-breakfast (ask for a list at the Tourist Centres in Norwich or Wells) - then take long, unhurried days out with a packed lunch, wind-cheaters and stout shoes.

The Youth Hostels Association is another excellent and inexpensive way for families with children to stop a while and explore the countryside, especially as now many hostels have specially eqipped annexes or dormitory accommodation which a complete family, including children under five, can have to themselves, coming and going as they please.

There must be very few indeed who don't know about the **YHA** but in case you are one of these rare souls the Association, which has been going now for about 56 years is a non-profit making organisation run by and for its members, and was created to give people, especially the young, the chance to find out more about the countryside by providing inexpensive places to stay. Lately it has put on a fresh face and the rather pious 'lights out at ten, walkers only' image has completely disappeared. You can travel by car, water, feet or any way you like. Accommodation, always in beautiful and/or interesting places, ranges from cottages to castles, mills to mansions and runs from the most basic (possibly the most fun to stay at) to the near-luxurious, with food to match. Some hostels lie along hidden tracks, others are modern and purpose-built and situated in cities, such as the one in Norwich, and have every modern convenience.

It is possible to join the YHA if you happen to come across a hostel you'd like to stay at there and then, but it's less chancy, specially in the holiday seasons to join before you go and to book ahead. Membership ranges from £2 to £5 p.a. according to age, and there is a special family subscription.

The nice thing about the YHA is that you meet all sorts of like-minded people from all over the world in a friendly and unsophisticated atmosphere, and friendships can be made that could very well last a lifetime.

When you receive your membership card you will also be sent various publications about what's going on in the hostels in the area you are visiting, such as the "Friendly Face Weekends". These could include, for instance, boat tours of the Hickling Nature Reserve, plus pub lunch and a Sunday lunch. Or a natural history weekend with walks, talks and slides of East Anglian flora and fauna at Brandon. Sometimes the hostel at Great Yarmouth offers a weekend on the Breydon Water Nature Reserve with slide shows and guided tours, while at Hunstanton you might find the theme would be coastal birds and their environment as you explore the sand-dunes and marshlands with a guide.

43

The themes and venues are constantly changing and in some of these, families of four or more pay a specially reduced rate. But remember for these you must already be a YHA member and it's always better to book ahead.

And for something rather different from the other places mentioned: at **MANNINGTON HALL GARDENS** - eighteen miles north of Norwich between Aylsham and Holt, a new Nature Trail was opened in the grounds in 1984. This takes you through meadows, fields and woodland - a walk full of discovery and delight, where you may find all sorts of unexpected flora and fauna if you step carefully and wear your eyes and ears on stalks.

The Gardens themselves are a paradise for lovers of roses and sweet-scented flowers and you won't go hungry for on weekdays during the season you will find coffee, lunches and light snacks on sale, while on Sundays there are cream teas. Mannington Hall itself belongs to, and is still lived in, by the descendants of Horatio Walpole, whose letters gave such a graphic picture of Georgian England. He bought it in about 1740, and it is open to the public by prior arrangement with the present owners.

NORWICH YOUTH HOSTEL 112, Turner Road, Norwich, Tel: Norwich 627647, conveniently placed for the city centre and all its delights.

SHERINGHAM YOUTH HOSTEL, 1, Cremer's Drift, Sheringham NR26 8HX Tel: Sheringham 823215

GREAT YARMOUTH YOUTH HOSTEL 2, Sandown Road, Great Yarmouth, in the centre of the town. It makes a good stepping-off spot for exploring the Norfolk Broads, as well as for Great Yarmouth itself.

NATIONAL TRUST ACORN CAMPS Richard Sneyd (Junior Division), The National Trust, P.O.Box 12, Westbury, Wiltshire, BA13 4NA. Tel: Westbury 826302.

YOUNG NATIONAL TRUST GROUP Norwich Area: Roger Chamberlain, Norwood, Sustead Road, Lower Gresham, Norfolk NR11 8RE Tel: Matlaske 394

BRANCASTER STAITHE CYCLE HIRE SCHEME Open Easter. May-September 10a.m.-6p.m. National Trust Information Centre, Brancaster Staithe. Tel: Brancaster 210719. If closed apply to DIAL HOUSE adjacent.

SCOLT HEAD NATIONAL NATURE RESERVE (Owned by National Trust and managed by the Nature Conservancy Council) Open all year. Warden: Brancaster Staithe Tel: Brancaster 210330.

BLAKENEY POINT NATURE RESERVE (National Trust) Open all year.

CLEY VISITOR CENTRE Open April-October, Tuesday-Sunday 10a.m.-5p.m.

MANNINGTON HALL GARDENS Open Sundays from May-September, 2-5 p.m. Wednesday, Thursday, Friday from June-August, 11a.m.-6 p.m.

NELSON COUNTRY

Horatio Nelson was born at Burnham Thorpe in 1758. The village, one of a charming and unspoiled cluster - all Burnhams of one kind or another - is about five miles west of Wells-next-the-Sea, and if you would like him brought to life you can't do better than pay a visit to Les Winter.

Les runs the 'Nelson' pub at Burnham Thorpe, and Nelson, his life and times, have obsessed him since taking it over in the 1960s. Before then Les had been a successful pig-farmer, and as far as he was concerned Nelson was just a name in a history book. However, once he became involved with the pub it seemed that he also became invaded by the spirit of that great Naval commander. As he explains: "It was as if Nelson was urging me to bring him back to life."

So with tremendous care and devotion, using much of the original fabric and fittings which had remained in what was up to then an almost derelict building, Les restored the place to its original state, a simple bar-parlour, smoky-dark, with high-backed wooden settles where private matters could be discussed among friends.

The talks that Les Winter gives about Nelson in the old tap-room, out of hours, are becoming a sought-after event with boys and girls all over the country, as well as the local children, but they're so popular that you need to write to him in advance to find out what's what if you would like your own family to take part.

The walls of the 'Nelson' constitute a complete exhibition of Nelsonia. There are paintings, illustrations from ancient picture-books and magazines, old menus, letters, broadsheets from the time of Trafalgar, and many other objects passed down from those times. In fact Les's collection, plus a further room of memorabilia which he will only show you when he gets to know you.

Les lives, talks and breathes Nelson. He even looks a little like him, having lost an eye himself. He has written one Nelson book and is now involved in further research and people continue to send him material from all over the world. Les will tell you that it was in this very pub that Nelson gave a dinner-party the night before joining Agamemnon to celebrate his promotion to captain in 1793. A very special evening it was, for he never returned to the village after than.

You'll pass muster with Les if you show that you have a true love of history, of the sea and of these parts - and know a little about his hero too. Bus loads of tourists doing the area are not his favourites, and he might very well tell them so!

This is all Nelson country, for it's among the tiny creeks and inlets which thread between the Burnhams Thorpe, Staithe, Market and Overy - loveliest of

In fact, Nelsonia is to be found all over Norfolk. The display of memorabilia is at the Maritime Museum at Great Yarmouth (see page 14), and you may catch a day when you can climb the Norfolk Pillar – the county's own Nelson's Column.

all - that Nelson probably first became aware of ships that sailed along them stealthily from the North Sea, bearing who knows what secrets. It made him realise the threat from invading forces this could mean, and fired his ambition to make the sea his career.

While ashore and waiting for a command (for during the 1780s he was pensioned off on half pay) you might have spotted Nelson sitting on the wall of the little harbour at Burnham Overy Staithe, perhaps with a book in his hand, perhaps waiting peacefully for the stage-coach to arrive from Norwich with the newspapers.

The church of All Saints, Burnham Thorpe, set in sweet green fields edged with Queen Anne's Lace in summer, is quite a step from the village. Nelson's father was Rector of Burnham Thorpe and both Nelson's parents, as well as his brother and sister, are buried in the church. Beneath the memorial to his father in the chancel stands a bust of Nelson who expected to be buried at Burnham Thorpe too. But it was not to be; he lies in St. Paul's Cathedral. However, you will find his signature in the marriage register when he was a witness to a friend's marriage, and the lectern and crucifix are made from timbers of his flagship Victory. There are kneeler cushions in the sanctuary embroidered with HMS Victory in full sail, and on the anniversary of the Battle of Trafalgar the white ensign, a full-size replica of the flag flown on the Victory at that battle, is flown from the church's fifteenth century tower. The original flag still remains inside the church.

The Burnham villages are full of echoes of England's naval hero. Not only in the pub names: The Victory, The Trafalgar, The Nelson, The Hero - but in the legends that abound - and who's to say they're not true. There's the yew-tree, still growing in Burnham Thorpe churchyard, which the boy Nelson is said to have climbed at midnight as a dare, returning with a bit of the tree to prove to his friends that he really did it. The pond in the vicarage garden (the actual house where Nelson was born has long been demolished, alas, but a plaque remains) which he is thought to have dug while he was at home on holiday. The huge flint barn by the pub where, some locals insist, he was actually born - his mother just being unable to get home in time!